D0856081

GLUTTONY

A DICTIONARY FOR THE INDULGENT

JENNIFER M. WOOD

Avon, Massachusetts

Published by
Adams Media, a division of F+W Media, Inc.
57 Littlefield Street, Avon, MA 02322. U.S.A.
www.adamsmedia.com

ISBN 10: 1-4405-2805-5
ISBN 13: 978-1-4405-2805-7
eISBN 10: 1-4405-2833-0
eISBN 13: 978-1-4405-2833-0

Printed in the United States of America.

10 9 8 7 6 5 4 3 2 1

Library of Congress Cataloging-in-Publication Data
is available from the publisher.

This publication is designed to provide accurate and authoritative
information with regard to the subject matter covered. It is sold
with the understanding that the publisher is not engaged in
rendering legal, accounting, or other professional advice. If legal
advice or other expert assistance is required, the services of a
competent professional person should be sought.

—From a *Declaration of Principles* jointly adopted
by a Committee of the American Bar Association
and a Committee of Publishers and Associations

Many of the designations used by manufacturers and sellers to
distinguish their product are claimed as trademarks. Where
those designations appear in this book and Adams Media was
aware of a trademark claim, the designations have been printed
with initial capital letters.

Illustration © clipart.com

*This book is available at quantity discounts for bulk purchases.
For information, please call 1-800-289-0963.*

An Introduction to

Gluttony

gluttony
(GLUHT-n-ee)
NOUN: Excessive indulgence in food and drink.

When one succumbs to the all-consuming temptation to indulge, there really is no resisting the yearning for more. Like Ciacco damned to the third circle in Dante's *Divine Comedy* or Tolkien's Shelob channeling the human desire to devour it all, this particular vice can weigh heavily on the soul and create an insatiable hunger that ultimately leads to one's destruction. The wants and well-being of others are secondary when overindulgence clogs the mind with insatiable thoughts. While gluttony is defined best in the demanding cry for more, this delightful dictionary gives a good taste of the most debaucherous sin.

A

abandon

(uh-BAN-duhn)

NOUN: A lack of restraint or inhibition.

> *Consuming plateful after plateful, Joseph ABANDONED any sense of restraint as he feasted on the delicious spread before him.*

absinthe

(AB-sinth)

NOUN: A highly alcoholic green liqueur made from wormwood.

abundance

(uh-BUN-duhnts)

NOUN: A great quantity of something; plentiful.

ad infinitum

(ad in-fi-NEYE-tum)

ADVERB: Literally translating to "to infinity," *ad infinitum* is usually used in the context of repeating a process or series of steps to infinity.

ad nauseam

(ad NAW-zee-um)

ADVERB: To an annoying or sickening degree.

adipose

(AD-uh-pohs)

ADJECTIVE: Pertaining to or containing fat.

adulation

(ad-yoo-LAY-shun)

NOUN: Extreme admiration, especially that which is disproportionate to what is deserving.

ample

(AM-puhl)

ADJECTIVE: As much or more than is required of something, in terms of size or quantity.

animalistic

(ann-uh-muh-LIST-ic)

NOUN: One who is preoccupied with animal—or sensual—needs as opposed to spiritual ones.

apolaustic

(app-oh-LAW-stick)

ADJECTIVE: Devoted to pleasure and enjoyment.

With a complete disregard of responsibility and social grace, the young socialite spent her time at the party indulging in APOLAUSTIC behavior, focusing more on finishing champagne bottles than conversations with her parents' acquaintances.

Gluttony and lust are

the only sins that abuse

something that is essential

to our survival.

—HENRY FAIRLIE

appetence
(AP-ih-tuhns)
NOUN: Strong craving or appetite, inclination, or
tendency.

appetite
(AP-ih-tahyt)
NOUN: Hunger or craving for something; often used
to describe one's desire for food.

appetition
(ap-ih-TISH-un)
NOUN: A desire or longing for something.

ardent
(ARH-dent)
ADJECTIVE: Passionate or eager.

> *Jules liked to refer to herself as an ARDENT*
> *connoisseur of wine and used it as an excuse to enjoy it*
> *whenever she wanted.*

avidity
(uh-VID-ih-tee)
NOUN: Strong enthusiasm toward or greediness for
something.

B

bacchanalian

(back-uh-NAIL-yuhn)

ADJECTIVE: Drunken and carousing.

banquet

(BANG-kwit)

NOUN: An elaborate meal, often held in honor of a specific person or occasion.

batterie de cuisine

(bat-uh-REE duh kwee-ZEEN)

NOUN: A French phrase meaning cooking utensils or vessels.

beefy

(BEEF-ee)

ADJECTIVE: Strong or muscular.

bender

(BEN-der)

NOUN: A protracted drinking binge.

> *Ironically, Shane missed his first day of work when a couple of cocktails to celebrate his new job turned into a three-day BENDER.*

besotted
(bih-SOTT-ed)
ADJECTIVE: Foolish as the result of something, such as love, money, or—most often—alcohol; drunk.

bibulous
(BIB-yuh-luss)
ADJECTIVE: Having a tendency to drink too much.

binge
(binj)
NOUN: A period of uncontrolled eating or drinking.

bite
(bahyt)
NOUN: A small amount of food.

blatant
(BLAYT-ent)
ADJECTIVE: Excessively obvious or conspicuous; flagrant.

Gluttony is an emotional

escape, a sign something

is eating us.

—Peter De Vries

blather

(BLATH-er)
VERB: To speak at length in a foolish manner;
babble.

blubber

(BLUHB-er)
NOUN: Excess body fat.

> *The corpulent woman's underarm BLUBBER sagged as
> she reached over her neighbor's plate, almost dragging
> her fat through his food.*

bolt

(bohlt)
VERB: To gobble up or chew food in a hurried
manner.

bon vivant

(BON vee-VAHNT)
NOUN: One who lives the good life, particularly as it
relates to food and drink. Also called a *bon viveur.*

> *A true BON VIVANT, Katherine spent the last year
> traveling the world indulging in the local delicacies of
> every stop.*

bottomless
(BOT-uhm-liss)
ADJECTIVE: Unlimited or without end; unending.

His stein appeared BOTTOMLESS since every time he finished his drink the bartender was there to immediately refill it.

bountiful
(BOUN-tih-ful)
ADJECTIVE: In large supply; plentiful.

braggadocio
(brag-uh-DOH-shee-oh)
NOUN: Boasting or bragging; a person who boasts or brags endlessly.

braggart
(BRAG-ert)
NOUN: A person who brags or boasts often.

brawny
(BRAWN-ee)
ADJECTIVE: Big or muscular; strapping.

In love, as in gluttony,

pleasure is a matter of the

utmost precision.

—Italo Calvino

bulky

(BUHL-kee)

ADJECTIVE: Large and cumbersome; broad or heavy.

burst

(burst)

VERB: To bust or break open in a forceful, violent, and usually unintentional manner; erupt.

buzz

(buzz)

NOUN: A feeling of pleasure or excitement that can be related to a positive experience or accomplishment or light intoxication.

Excess of liberty, whether it

lies in state or individuals,

seems only to pass into

excess of slavery.

—Plato

C

capacity
(kuh-PASS-ih-tee)
NOUN: The maximum amount of something that can be held; the ability to do something.

carouse
(kuh-ROWZ)
VERB: To take part in a loud or rowdy social activity, typically one involving alcohol.

It is well known that CAROUSING with Mitchell is an all-night affair, with more toasting and drinking in one evening than most do in one year.

chock full
(CHOHK ful)
ADJECTIVE: Filled to the brim; bursting.

chock-a-block
(CHOHK-uh-blohk)
ADJECTIVE: Filled to capacity; squeezed together.

There is a difference

between eating and

drinking for strength and

from mere gluttony.

—HENRY DAVID THOREAU

chowhound
(CHOU-hound)
NOUN: A person who thoroughly enjoys food and eating.

chubby
(CHUB-ee)
ADJECTIVE: Heavy or plump.

chunky
(CHUNG-kee)
ADJECTIVE: Stout or stocky.

complacent
(kuhm-PLAY-cent)
ADJECTIVE: Self-satisfied in such a way that one becomes unaware of potential dangers or changes; smug.

compulsive
(kuhm-PUHL-siv)
ADJECTIVE: An excessive need or desire that seems to be motivated by some internal force.

connoisseur

(kon-uh-SOHR)

NOUN: One who has developed an expertise or is a specialist in some field or artistic endeavor; an expert.

consumption

(kohn-SUMP-shun)

NOUN: The act of consuming or utilizing something; the word is often used in reference to food or eating.

contentment

(kohn-TENT-muhnt)

NOUN: A state of feeling satisfied; gratification.

After the holiday feast, the sound of CONTENTMENT filled the room as everyone sat quietly and digested the delicious food they just devoured.

continual

(kuhn-TIN-yoo-ul)

ADJECTIVE: Continuing frequently and on a regular basis; without interruption.

copious

(KOH-pee-us)

ADJECTIVE: A large amount; abundant.

The family fully expected everyone to celebrate and indulge after their daughter's wedding, so they made sure COPIOUS amounts of alcohol were on hand at the reception for the bride and groom.

cormorant

(COR-mer-ehnt)

NOUN: A type of voracious seabird, *cormorant* is also used in reference to a greedy person.

cornucopia

(korn-yuh-COE-pee-uh)

NOUN: From Latin, *cornucopia* means "horn of plenty" but has come to describe any sort of overabundance.

corpulent

(KORP-you-lunt)

ADJECTIVE: Obese or fat.

Nothing exceeds like excess.

—AL JOURGENSEN

cosset
(KOS-it)
VERB: To pamper or coddle a person or thing.

covetous
(KUHV-ih-tuss)
ADJECTIVE: Feeling extreme greed or desire, especially to possess those things belonging to someone else.

cram
(kram)
VERB: To eat very quickly and voraciously; to fill something to capacity.

> *Still sitting long after the others left, the pudgy little boy CRAMMED every morsel of food left on the table into his mouth.*

crapulous
(KRAP-yuh-luss)
ADJECTIVE: Describes a person or thing who makes a habit of overindulging in food and/or alcohol; the word also describes one who is suffering from the effects of overindulgence.

craving
(KREY-ving)
NOUN: A strong desire or longing for something.

cropsick
(KROP-sik)
NOUN: A feeling of sickness as the result of overindulgence in food and/or alcohol.

D

debauchery

(dih-BOCH-er-ee)

NOUN: Self-indulgent behavior, usually of an immoral kind; licentiousness.

> *As one drink led to another and another after that, Kevin lost all good judgment and became involved in some of the DEBAUCHERY happening around him.*

decadence

(DEK-uh-dunce)

NOUN: *Decadence* can be used in reference to either a state of moral decline or one of extreme self-indulgence; debauchery.

decadent

(DEK-uh-dent)

ADJECTIVE: Describes something marked by decadence; self-indulgent or immoral.

decant

(dih-KANT)

VERB: To pour wine or another liquid from one container to another in order to avoid disturbing sediment.

To describe drunkenness

for the colorful vocabulary

is rather cynical. There

is nothing easier than to

capitalize on drunkards.

—ANTON CHEKHOV

delectable

(de-LEK-tuh-bull)

ADJECTIVE: Extremely enjoyable or delightful, the word is often used in reference to food.

> *After the DELECTABLE meal Roger feasted on, he could not resist disregarding proper table manners and licking each of his fat fingers.*

deluge

(DELL-yoodje)

NOUN: Often used in reference to a flood, *deluge* can be used in reference to anything of which there is an overwhelming amount.

deluxe

(duh-LUX)

ADJECTIVE: Luxurious or sumptuous.

demand

(duh-MAND)

VERB: To request something in a firm or urgent manner.

desirous

(dih-ZAHYR-uhs)

ADJECTIVE: To desire or wish for something.

dessert
(dez-ERT)
NOUN: A sweet course eaten at the end of a meal.

devour
(dih-VOUR)
VERB: To eat or consume something quickly and voraciously.

dine
(dahyn)
VERB: To eat or consume a meal, particularly dinner.

dipsomania
(dip-suh-MAY-nee-uh)
NOUN: A regular and uncontrollable craving for alcohol.

disproportionate
(dis-pruh-PAWR-shun-it)
ADJECTIVE: Out of proportion or unequal; uneven.

If the DISPROPORTIONATE slice he cut himself was not indication enough, Reuben could not stop talking about how much he loved the decadent chocolate cake he bought for everyone attending his dinner party to enjoy.

31

dissipation
(dis-uh-PEY-shuhn)
NOUN: Overindulgence, particularly in regards to alcohol; the lessening or disappearance of something.

down
(doun)
VERB: To gulp or guzzle food or drink in a quick or greedy manner.

drink
(dringk)
VERB: To take in any liquid, though it is often used in reference to the habitual intake of alcohol.

drinkable
(DRINGK-uh-buhl)
ADJECTIVE: Any liquid that can be safely consumed; *drinkable* as a noun also refers to an enjoyable beverage.

Vices are sometimes only

virtues carried to excess.

—CHARLES DICKENS

drunk

(druhngk)

NOUN: An alcoholic.

> *The red-nosed DRUNK bellied up to the bar hoping the barkeep would forget about his outstanding tab; but, unfortunately for the drunk and fortunately for the other patrons, the bartender sent him right back outside.*

drunk tank

(druhngk tank)

NOUN: A special area or cell of a jail or police station reserved for those who have been arrested for public intoxication.

drunkard

(DRUHNGK-erd)

NOUN: A habitual drinker; alcoholic.

drunken

(DRUHNGK-en)

ADJECTIVE: Intoxicated; of, involving, or occurring during intoxication.

But one can be a cannibal

and still be honourable,

just as one can be a glutton

and still be honest.

One does not exclude

the other.

—Conseil in Jules Verne's
*Twenty Thousand Leagues
Under the Sea* (1869)

E

eat

(eet)

VERB: To consume something, particularly food.

ebriety

(ee-BRAHY-ih-tee)

NOUN: A state of intoxication.

ecstatic

(eck-STAT-ick)

ADJECTIVE: Describes a feeling of great delight, even rapture.

> *Each and every sugary swirl atop and along the three-tier cake made the chubby little children ECSTATIC as they drooled over their empty plates waiting for their mother to cut into the creative confection.*

edacious

(ih-DEY-shuhs)

ADJECTIVE: Voracious or gluttonous.

edible

(ED-uh-buhl)

ADJECTIVE: Describes something that is safe to be eaten.

effusive
(ih-FYOO-siv)
ADJECTIVE: Extravagant or overly expressive; overenthusiastic.

embellish
(em-BEL-ish)
VERB: To exaggerate or enhance something by creating details that might not be true.

emphatic
(em-FA-tik)
ADJECTIVE: Characterized by emphasis; forceful.

endless
(END-lis)
ADJECTIVE: Without end or limits; never-ending.

englut
(en-GLUHT)
VERB: To gulp or gobble down; devour.

engorge
(en-GAWRJ)
VERB: To gorge oneself with food; to eat greedily.

enormous

(ih-NAWR-muhs)

ADJECTIVE: Exceedingly large or immense; huge.

enthusiasm

(en-THOO-zee-az-uhm)

NOUN: Passionate interest or excitement about
something.

enthusiast

(en-THOO-zee-ist)

NOUN: One who is extremely passionate or excited
about a particular interest.

epicure

(EP-ih-kyoor)

NOUN: One who has developed a refined taste for
food and/or drink; gourmet.

> *The paper's critic was a true EPICURE, as her
> sharp palate could taste the slightest error even the
> most acclaimed chef might make during a dish's
> preparation—and then she would go on to humble him
> with her poisoned pen.*

esurient
(ih-SOOR-ee-uhnt)
ADJECTIVE: Greedy; hungry.

exaggerate
(eg-ZAJ-uhr-eyt)
VERB: To overstate something; embellish.

exceed
(ek-SEED)
VERB: To surpass or go beyond the expected limits of something; excel.

excess
(EK-sess)
NOUN: A surplus of something; overindulgence.

excessive
(ek-SESS-iv)
ADJECTIVE: Typically used in a negative manner, *excessive* means something that goes beyond what is considered necessary or proper.

Excess of joy is harder to

bear than any amount

of sorrow.

—Honoré de Balzac

exorbitant

(egg-ZORE-bih-tunt)

ADJECTIVE: Greater than what is reasonable; extreme or excessive.

> *Many are astonished at the EXORBITANT prices the bistro charges for such tiny plates, but the big tastes from the best ingredients makes indulging on the smaller portions worth every last cent.*

extravagance

(ek-STRAV-uh-guhnz)

NOUN: Something that is excessive or unnecessary; expensive or wasteful.

extreme

(ek-STREEM)

ADJECTIVE: To an exceeding degree; going beyond what is normal or necessary.

exuberant

(ig-ZOO-burr-uhnt)

ADJECTIVE: Extremely enthusiastic; high-spirited.

exult

(ig-ZULT)

VERB: To celebrate or revel.

> *The feast was meant to EXULT the recent conquering of the neighboring land, with the king allowing even the peasants to come and taste the many dishes his kitchen had prepared.*

F

famished

(FAM-isht)

ADJECTIVE: Starving or hungry.

farctate

(FARK-tayt)

ADJECTIVE: Stuffed or filled from overeating; the opposite of hollow.

> *Julie sat there, immobilized and FARCTATE, after finally finishing the seven-course meal her fiancé's mother put together to celebrate their engagement.*

fat

(fat)

ADJECTIVE: Overweight.

feast

(feest)

NOUN: A large or sumptuous meal; a thing that provides immense pleasure, as in a *feast* for the senses.

feed

(feed)

VERB: To give food to a person or animal.

felicity

(fih-LISS-ih-tee)

NOUN: Extreme happiness or satisfaction; bliss.

fervent

(FER-vunt)

ADJECTIVE: Extremely enthusiastic or passionate; ardent.

filled

(filld)

ADJECTIVE: Full with food or another substance.

flab

(flab)

NOUN: Refers to the excess fat on one's body.

flagrant

(FLAY-gruhnt)

ADJECTIVE: Extremely obvious or blatant.

flambé
(flom-BAY)
VERB: A style of culinary preparation where alcohol, such as brandy, is poured over a food item and set aflame in order to give the food more flavor.

fleshy
(FLESH-ee)
ADJECTIVE: An abundance of flesh; plump.

flood
(flud)
VERB: To arrive in overwhelming amounts or quanities.

fondness
(FOND-niss)
NOUN: Affection or liking for or toward something.

Some times a FONDNESS for the finer things in life can result in both empty pockets and expanded waistlines.

Excess of liberty, whether it

lies in state or individuals,

seems only to pass into

excess of slavery.

—PLATO

foodie
(FOO-dee)
NOUN: One who shows great enthusiasm toward food—both preparing and consuming it.

foofaraw
(FOO-fuh-raw)
NOUN: Much fussing over a trivial, unimportant matter.

forage
(FOR-uj)
VERB: To search or hunt for food or provisions.

frenetically
(fruh-NET-ik-lee)
ADVERB: In a frenzied or feverish manner.

frenzy
(FREN-zee)
NOUN: A state of extreme excitement or agitation.

> *When it came time to move on to the dessert course, there was nearly a feeding FRENZY as the guests crowded around the table with the various tasty confections.*

full

(fuhl)

ADJECTIVE: A person or object that is filled to capacity.

G

galore
(guh-LORE)
ADJECTIVE: Describes something that is in abundance; plentiful.

gamut
(GAM-ut)
NOUN: The entire range or extent.

gargantuan
(gahr-GAN-choo-uhn)
ADJECTIVE: Gigantic; enormous.

garner
(GAR-nur)
VERB: To receive or acquire.

gas
(gas)
NOUN: An informal name for flatulence.

gastric
(GA-strik)
ADJECTIVE: Of or relating to the stomach.

gastronome
(GAS-truh-nohm)
NOUN: A connoisseur of fine food; gourmet.

generous
(JENN-er-uss)
ADJECTIVE: *Generous* can describe a charitable, giving person; *generous* can also refer to something that is very large in size.

> *Not one to resist, Michael made sure he received a very GENEROUS portion of the turkey as it was passed around the table.*

the gimmes
(thuh GIM-eez)
NOUN: The expectation or demand that others be charitable and giving toward someone; greediness.

girth
(gerth)
NOUN: The width or circumference of something; *girth* can also be a nicer word for fat.

glob
(glob)
NOUN: A lump; a drop of liquid.

globular

(GLOB-yoo-lar)

ADJECTIVE: In the shape of a globe; spherical.

glut

(gluht)

VERB: To eat until one is satiated or to eat to excess.

glutton

(GLUHT-en)

NOUN: One who eats or drinks excessively; *glutton* can also be used more broadly in reference to someone who does anything to excess, such as a *glutton* for punishment.

gluttonous

(GLUHT-en-uhs)

ADJECTIVE: Eating or drinking to excess; insatiable.

gnaw

(naw)

VERB: To bite or chew on something persistently.

gobble
(GOB-uhl)
VERB: To eat something in a greedy, hurried manner; guzzle.

gorge
(gawrj)
VERB: To eat to excess; devour.

> *Even though she had eaten only a few hours before, Katherine did not give pause at the dinner table and proceeded to GORGE on everything offered.*

gormandize
(GAWR-muhn-dahyz)
VERB: To eat something in a greedy, gluttonous manner.

gourmand
(goor-MAHND)
NOUN: One who loves food, so eats well and to excess.

gourmet
(goor-MEY)
NOUN: An expert on fine food and drink.

O gluttony, it is to thee we

owe our griefs!

—Geoffrey Chaucer

gratuitous
(gruh-TOO-ih-tuss)
ADJECTIVE: Given or done free of charge.

grease
(grees)
NOUN: Melted animal fat.

greed
(greed)
NOUN: An intense desire to possess as much as possible.

greediness
(GREED-ee-nuhs)
NOUN: Characterized by greed or gluttony.

gulosity
(gyoo-LOS-ih-tee)
NOUN: Gluttony or greediness.

gulp

(guhlp)

VERB: To swallow something quickly or hungrily.

Drink after drink, Martin did not bother sipping or slowly drinking his favorite spirit; instead, he GULPED down the whiskey without a second thought.

gusto

(GUHS-toh)

NOUN: Enthusiasm or hearty enjoyment.

guttle

(GUHT-l)

VERB: To eat in a greedy manner; devour.

guzzle

(GUHZ-uhl)

VERB: To drink something quickly or in abundance.

A gourmet

is just a glutton

with brains.

—PHILIP W. HABERMAN, JR.

H

hangover

(HANG-oh-ver)

NOUN: The aftereffect of indulging in drugs or alcohol, which is often marked by nausea, a headache, and general listlessness.

> *It was a rather simple cycle that kept the drunkard anywhere from sober: Every morning when he woke up with a HANGOVER, he would reach for the nearest bottle in order to drink away the pain.*

hanker

(HANG-ker)

VERB: To have a persistent desire or longing for something.

haute cuisine

(oht kwee-ZEEN)

NOUN: Gourmet cooking; *haute cuisine* can also refer to the art of food preparation.

> *In order to enjoy HAUTE CUISINE, one must have a fairly expanded palate, as what's trendy today will likely taste very different from whatever is in next week.*

heavy

(HEV-ee)

ADJECTIVE: Describes something that weighs a lot, including a person.

hedonist
(HEE-duh-nist)
NOUN: A person who dedicates his or her life completely to the pursuit of pleasure.

hefty
(HEFF-tee)
ADJECTIVE: Describes something that is large in size, weight, or amount—from a person to a sum of money; heavy to lift.

high living
(hahy LIV-ing)
NOUN: Hedonism or self-indulgence.

hog
(hawg)
VERB: To act in a greedy or selfish manner.

holus-bolus
(HOH-lus BOH-lus)
ADVERB: All at once; altogether.

The chief beginning of evil is

goodness in excess.

—Menander

hunger

(HUHNG-ger)

NOUN: A need or want for something, including food; as a verb, it means to feel a need or want for something.

hungry

(HUHNG-gree)

ADJECTIVE: Needing or wanting something, especially food.

I

ice cream

(AHYS kreem)

NOUN: A frozen dessert usually made from milk or cream and sugar, and flavored in various ways.

icebox

(AHYS-boks)

NOUN: An insulated storage unit used to keep food and beverages cool.

icing

(AHY-sing)

NOUN: A sugary spread used on cakes, cookies, and other baked goods; frosting.

idle

(AHYD-l)

ADJECTIVE: Inactive; lazy.

VERB: To do nothing; to sit around aimlessly.

ill

(il)

NOUN: The state of feeling sick; unwell.

imbibe
(im-BIBE)
VERB: To take something in or drink something, especially alcohol.

immeasurable
(ih-MEZH-er-uh-bull)
ADJECTIVE: A quantity not able to be measured; vast.

immense
(ih-MENS)
ADJECTIVE: Vast or huge; immeasurable or boundless.

immoderation
(ih-mod-uhr-AY-shun)
NOUN: A lack of moderation; excess.

incisor
(in-SAHY-zer)
NOUN: Any tooth meant for cutting or gnawing; humans have four at the front of their mouths.

How easy for those who do

not bulge to not overindulge!

—OGDEN NASH

indefatigable
(in-duh-FAT-ih-guh-buhl)
ADJECTIVE: Unable to fatigue; untiring.

indulgence
(in-DUHL-juhns)
NOUN: The act of indulging yourself or someone else; a luxury.

> *For some it's rich chocolate, others a fine wine, and some a thick-cut steak—everyone has their culinary INDULGENCE.*

inebriated
(in-EE-bree-ate-ud)
ADJECTIVE: Drunk or intoxicated.

inexorable
(in-EK-sur-uh-buhl)
ADJECTIVE: Unable to be moved or persuaded; unalterable.

infinite
(IN-fuh-nit)
ADJECTIVE: Without any measurable limits or end; immeasurable.

infuse

(in-FYUZE)

VERB: To fill or instill; to penetrate or soak.

ingluvious

(in-GLOO-vee-uhs)

ADJECTIVE: Gluttonous.

inordinate

(in-OR-den-it)

ADJECTIVE: An excessive amount; immoderate.

insatiable

(in-SEY-shuh-buhl)

ADJECTIVE: Unable to be satisfied; insatiate.

> *To the wait staff, the patron sitting in the corner booth seemed downright INSATIABLE, finishing off plate after plate without pause.*

intemperance

(in-TEM-per-uhns)

NOUN: A lack of self-control; the gratification of an excessive desire, especially one for alcohol.

The miser and the glutton

are two facetious buzzards:

one hides his store, and the

other stores his hide.

—Josh Billings

intoxicated

(in-TOK-si-kay-ted)

ADJECTIVE: Drunk; overly excited or happy to the point of acting foolish.

irrepressible

(ir-ih-PRES-uh-buhl)

ADJECTIVE: Uncontrollable; unable to be restrained.

irresistible

(ir-re-ZIS-tuh-buhl)

ADJECTIVE: Impossible to resist; extremely appealing.

itch

(ich)

NOUN: A strong, restless desire.

J

Gluttony demands a heavy

tribute but gives the basest

returns: the more delicate

the food, the more reeking

the dung.

—Pope Innocent III

jam-pack
(JAM-pak)
VERB: To fill to capacity or pack as tightly as possible; to crowd.

jaunt
(jawnt)
NOUN: A short journey taken for pleasure.

jigger
(JIG-er)
NOUN: A glass used to measure alcohol, usually approximately one and a half ounces.

jiggle
(JIG-uhl)
VERB: To move up and down in a short, jerky motion.

jones
(johnz)
VERB: To crave, usually referring to narcotics.

jovial

(JOH-vee-uhl)

ADJECTIVE: Characterized by a hearty sense of humor; jolly.

jowl

(joul)

NOUN: A fold of fatty flesh hanging under the neck.

The surly old professor was nicknamed Bulldog by his students due to his prominent JOWLS.

juicehead

(JOOS-hed)

NOUN: A heavy drinker.

K

katzenjammer
(KAT-suhn-jam-er)
NOUN: A hangover.

keg
(keg)
NOUN: A small barrel, usually containing five to ten gallons.

keister
(KEE-ster)
NOUN: Buttocks.

kill
(kil)
VERB: To eat or drink the last of something.

kitchen
(KICH-uhn)
NOUN: The room in the house where meals are prepared and usually consumed.

knock back

(nok bak)

VERB: To drink.

VERB: To gulp down a drink—especially an alcoholic one—quickly.

> *The regulars sat at the bar KNOCKING BACK drinks and laughing loudly; whatever problems they entered with would surely be forgotten, at least until the next morning.*

I am not a glutton—

I am an explorer of food.

—ERMA BOMBECK

L

large
(lahrj)

ADJECTIVE: Big in comparison to what it should be; overweight.

largess
(lar-JESS)

NOUN: Extreme generosity, but with a condescending air; charity.

lavish
(LAV-ish)

VERB: To spend excessive amounts of money; to give generous gifts.

With whispers circulating of the family's wealth dwindling, they held a party with a LAVISH spread of the finest foods in order to dispel what everyone else was saying.

lawless
(LAW-lis)

ADJECTIVE: Without law or without regard to the law; unruly.

laxity
(LAX-ih-tee)
NOUN: Carelessness; the state of being loose or slack.

libation
(li-BAY-shun)
NOUN: An alcoholic beverage.

liking
(LAHY-king)
NOUN: A fondness or tendency toward a particular thing or person; a feeling of pleasantness.

limitless
(LIM-it-les)
ADJECTIVE: Without limits or boundaries; infinite.

liqueur
(li-KER)
NOUN: A sweet-tasting alcoholic beverage.

longing

(LONG-ing)

NOUN: A strong desire for a person or thing that is often out of reach.

Lucullan

(loo-KULH-uhn)

ADJECTIVE: After the great Roman general and politician Lucullus and his lavish banquets, *Lucullan* means sumptuous or indulgent, especially with regard to food and drink.

luxuriate

(luhg-ZHOOR-ee-eyt)

VERB: To enjoy oneself and treat oneself to luxuries; to delight in.

luxurious

(luhg-ZHOOR-ee-us)

ADJECTIVE: Something marked by high quality; sumptuous.

> *Spending so much time in such a high-end kitchen, the chef came to forget what a LUXURIOUS ingredient truffle oil actually was and would use it without measuring or thinking twice in just about every dish.*

luxury

(LUGH-zhoor-ee)

NOUN: An unnecessary item that is extremely enjoyable, but never essential.

M

Glutton: one who digs his

grave with his teeth.

—FRENCH PROVERB

magniloquent

(mag-NIL-oh-kwuhnt)

ADJECTIVE: Pompous or boastful.

masticate

(MASS-tih-kate)

VERB: To grind or chew something with one's teeth; chomp.

maudlin

(MAWD-lin)

ADJECTIVE: Overly emotional or sentimental, often as the result of alcohol consumption.

> *While initially his overindulgence in the drink would bring out a very cheery side of Timothy, a more MAUDLIN man would appear during the wee hours of the night, almost near tears over his many laments.*

modus vivendi

(MO-duss vih-VEN-dee)

NOUN: A lifestyle; way of life.

munch
(munch)

VERB: To chew one's food with purpose—and often with accompanying sounds.

The spoiled little child sat in her chair MUNCHING away as the maid cleaned up the spills and messes she made during her meals.

munchies
(MUNCH-ees)

NOUN: Snacks; "to have the *munchies*" can also mean a desire for junk food.

munificent
(myoo-NIF-ih-sent)

ADJECTIVE: Extremely generous or giving.

N

GLUTTON, n.

A person who escapes the

evils of moderation by

committing dyspepsia.

—AMBROSE BIERCE

nausea
(NAW-zee-uh)
NOUN: Feeling sick to one's stomach with the urge to vomit.

nauseate
(NAW-zee-eyt)
VERB: To make someone feel nausea.

needless
(NEED-les)
ADJECTIVE: Unnecessary; pointless.

never-ending
(NEV-er-EN-ding)
ADJECTIVE: Not likely to ever end or stop; infinite.

nibble
(NIB-uhl)
VERB: To eat something with a series of small, delicate bites.

> *The queen made it a point to NIBBLE neatly on whatever she was eating whenever she was in front of people, but as her portly appearance could attest, she had no qualms about devouring whatever food was within reach whenever she was alone.*

nosh

(nosh)

VERB: To snack, particularly between meals. As a
noun, nosh refers to a snack.

numerous

(NOOM-er-uhs)

ADJECTIVE: Many; abundant.

> *NUMEROUS courses, NUMEROUS bottles,
> NUMEROUS servings—everything was in abundance
> whenever they gathered for a meal.*

obese

(oh-BEES)

ADJECTIVE: Morbidly fat or overweight.

oenophile

(EE-nuh-file)

NOUN: A connoisseur of fine wines.

> *For some reason Sophia considers herself a true OENOPHILE; she must not realize that constant consumption is not what makes one a connoisseur.*

omnivorous

(om-NIV-er-uhs)

ADJECTIVE: Eating both animal and vegetable foods.

opulent

(OP-yoo-lent)

ADJECTIVE: Characterized by wealth and expensive tastes.

outsized

(out-SAHYZD)

ADJECTIVE: Much larger than expected; enormous.

My regimen is lust and

avarice for exercise, gluttony

and sloth for relaxation.

—MASON COOLEY

overabundance

(OH-ver-uh-BUHN-duhns)

NOUN: A surplus or greater amount of something than what is needed.

overdo

(oh-ver-DOO)

VERB: To spoil something by letting it last too long or doing it too often.

overdrinking

(oh-ver-DRINGK-ing)

VERB: To drink too much.

overeat

(oh-ver-EET)

VERB: To eat too much, particularly if it's done habitually.

> *It might be typical to OVEREAT as a family during the holidays or on special occasions, but the Petersons choose to overindulge almost every night.*

overfeed

(oh-ver-FEED)

VERB: To feed a person or thing more than its normal intake.

overflow

(oh-ver-FLOH)

NOUN: The amount of something that is left over when something—like a container—is filled to its capacity. The phrase can also be used to describe a precarious emotional state where one is overwhelmed by his or her own feelings.

overgorge

(oh-ver-GORJ)

VERB: To indulge in something to excess.

overindulgent

(oh-ver-in-DUHL-jent)

ADJECTIVE: Prone to binging.

overstress

(oh-ver-STRESS)

VERB: To emphasize something too much; to inflict an excess of psychological strain on another person.

overweight

(oh-ver-WEYT)

ADJECTIVE: Weighing more than what is normal; fat.

overwhelm

(oh-ver-WELM)

VERB: To inundate a person or thing with too much of something; deluge.

> *The intense amount of garlic in the dish OVERWHELMED the rest of the flavors, and the breath of those who ate a plate of the pasta would overwhelm their dining companions.*

overzealous

(oh-ver-ZELL-us)

ADJECTIVE: Filled with intense enthusiasm or excitement.

P

packed
(pakt)
ADJECTIVE: Filled to capacity.

pamper
(PAM-per)
VERB: To indulge someone's desires, especially luxurious desires.

pantophagous
(pan-TOFF-uh-gus)
ADJECTIVE: Eating or requiring a wide variety of foods.

> *In order to satisfy the master's PANTOPHAGOUS appetite, the household employs three different chefs who specialize in different types of cuisines.*

penchant
(PEN-chent)
NOUN: Having a strong liking for something.

It is immoral to get drunk

because the headache comes

after the drinking, but if the

headache came first and the

drunkenness afterwards, it

would be moral to get drunk.

—SAMUEL BUTLER

perseverate

(per-SEV-ehr-eyt)

VERB: To continue repeating the same thing again and again.

piggish

(PIG-ish)

ADJECTIVE: Behaving like a pig by eating in a gluttonous manner or behaving in a generally stubborn way.

pleasure seeker

(PLEH-zhur SEEK-er)

NOUN: A person whose actions are motivated by the desire for pleasure; hedonist.

plenitude

(PLEN-ih-tood)

NOUN: An abundance of something.

plenteous

(PLEN-tee-uhs)

ADJECTIVE: An abundance; plentiful.

plentiful
(PLEN-tih-ful)
ADJECTIVE: In large supply.

plethora
(PLETH-er-uh)
NOUN: A large quantity of something; overabundance.

plump
(plump)
ADJECTIVE: Heavy or overweight; *plump* is often used in a more positive rather than derogatory manner.

> *Nathaniel's PLUMP little fingers served as the perfect spoon when he slyly scooped the last of the cookie batter from the baker's bowl.*

podgy
(PAWD-jee)
ADJECTIVE: Pudgy.

polydipsia
(pol-ee-DIP-see-uh)
NOUN: An unusually excessive thirst.

porcine
(PORE-sein)
ADJECTIVE: Resembling a pig in behavior or appearance.

portly
(PORT-lee)
ADJECTIVE: Generously proportioned, but wearing it well.

postprandial
(pohst-PRAN-dee-uhl)
ADJECTIVE: Something that occurs after a meal, particularly dinner.

potable
(POH-tuh-bull)
NOUN: A liquid that is safe to drink, particularly one made from alcohol.

It is not truly a party unless there are plenty of POTABLES and edibles available for everybody to enjoy.

prodigal
(PROD-ih-gul)
ADJECTIVE: Having or giving something on a lavish scale.

prodigious
(pro-DIDGE-uss)
ADJECTIVE: Large in size, impact, or stature; impressive.

profligate
(PROF-li-geyt)
ADJECTIVE: Excessively wasteful.

profuse
(proh-FYOOS)
ADJECTIVE: Abundant; extravagant.

prolific
(pruh-LIFF-ick)
ADJECTIVE: Present in large numbers or quantities; plentiful.

> *Thankfully the garden's strawberry plant was rather PROLIFIC, as Peter constantly plucked the ripe berries and popped them in his mouth whenever he passed by.*

propensity
(pruh-PEN-sit-ee)
NOUN: An inclination or tendency.

pudge
(pudj)
NOUN: A person who is short and chubby.

pyriform
(PEER-uh-form)
ADJECTIVE: Pear-shaped.

The pleasures of the palate

deal with us like the Egyptian

thieves, who strangle those

whom they embrace.

—SENECA

Q and R

quaff
(kwoff)
VERB: To drink something quickly and/or with relish.

quench
(kwench)
VERB: To satisfy one's thirst; to subdue something.

> *Nothing seemed to QUENCH the drunk's thirst as he continued drinking, not until he was full, but until he was passed out.*

rabid
(RAB-id)
ADJECTIVE: Referring to anything extreme or fanatical.

rampant
(RAM-punt)
ADJECTIVE: Widespread; out of control.

rapacious
(ruh-PAY-shus)
ADJECTIVE: Greedy; predatory.

rapacity
(ruh-PASS-ih-tee)
NOUN: Greed.

rapture
(RAP-shur)
NOUN: A state of euphoria or bliss; ecstasy.

ravenous
(RAV-uh-nuhs)
ADJECTIVE: Extremely hungry; greedy.

relish
(REL-ish)
VERB: To greatly enjoy something. *Relish* can also be used as a noun in reference to a moment of great enjoyment.

repress
(ree-PRESS)
VERB: Subdue; surpress.

revelry
(REV-el-ree)
NOUN: A noisy celebration that often includes excessive eating, drinking, and frivolity.

rife
(rahyf)
ADJECTIVE: Widespread and in abundant supply; endemic.

robust
(roh-BUST)
ADJECTIVE: Strong and rich in flavor or smell.

> *Robert's discernable palate and lack of tact are a terrible pairing—especially for the kitchen staff—as he will send back any dish lacking ROBUST flavor.*

rotund
(roh-TUND)
ADJECTIVE: Rounded or plump.

Covetousness is a sort

of mental gluttony, not

confined to money, but

greedy of honor and feeding

on selfishness.

—Nicholas Chamfort

S

I think it's important

to encourage gluttony

in all its formats.

—LYDIA LUNCH

sake
(SAH-kee)
NOUN: An alcoholic Japanese beverage made from fermented rice.

sangria
(sang-GREE-uh)
NOUN: A Spanish drink made of wine and fruit.

sapid
(SAP-id)
ADJECTIVE: Having a strong and agreeable taste.

> *That portly fellow eats in such haste that it does not matter whether the food is SAPID or even fully cooked.*

sated
(SEYT-ed)
ADJECTIVE: To be full or satisfied.

satiate
(SEY-shee-eyt)
VERB: To satisfy one's hunger; to indulge a person or thing.

satisfaction
(sat-iss-FAK-shuhn)
NOUN: The fulfillment of a need or desire or the feeling that accompanies that; contentment.

savor
(SEY-vuhr)
VERB: To enjoy something in an unhurried manner so as to let the experience last longer; relish.

> *When it comes to fowl straight off the rotisserie, Benjamin chooses to SAVOR each succulent bite, pulling the meat slowly from the bone and chewing each mouthful slowly.*

scoff
(skawf)
VERB: *Scoff* can mean to either show disdain for a person, thing, or idea or to eat one's food in a very quick and voracious manner.

self-centered
(self-SEN-tuhrd)
ADJECTIVE: To only be concerned with one's own selfish needs.

self-indulgence
(self-in-DUL-juhnts)
NOUN: To spoil oneself; to show a lack of self-control when it comes to indulging one's desires and passions.

selfish
(SELF-ish)
ADJECTIVE: Concerned with one's own needs and passions or behaving in a way that indicates you are only concerned with yourself.

shameless
(SHEYM-lis)
ADJECTIVE: Feeling a lack of embarrassment or humiliation in a situation where societal norms would call for it; unashamed.

shattered
(SHAT-erd)
ADJECTIVE: Most often used to describe something that has been broken into pieces, *shattered* can also describe someone who is drunk.

Sisyphean
(sis-uh-FEE-en)
ADJECTIVE: Endless work or labor, though often without a purpose.

slake
(sleyk)
VERB: To satisfy an appetite for something, particularly a desire for an alcoholic beverage.

slobber
(SLOB-er)
VERB: To drool or let saliva or some other liquid run from one's mouth.

> *While it's always polite to thank someone who has prepared a meal for you—SLOBBERING in anticipation is not the best way of going about offering your appreciation.*

smashed
(smasht)
ADJECTIVE: Extremely drunk.

Man is the only animal

which esteems itself rich in

proportion to the number

and voracity of its parasites.

—George Bernard Shaw

snack
(snack)
VERB: To eat a small amount of food in between regular meals; as a noun, a snack is a small amount of food you eat.

soak up
(sohk up)
VERB: The phrase really means to absorb something but is used more informally in reference to excessive drinking.

sop
(sop)
VERB: To dip or soak a piece of food in a liquid; absorb.

> *Once he cleaned all the food off of his plate, he used a piece of bread to SOP up the remaining juices of the steak.*

spendthrift
(SPEND-thrift)
NOUN: One who spends money in an extravagant, squandering manner.

spendy
(SPEN-dee)
ADJECTIVE: Expensive.

splurge
(splurj)
VERB: To indulge in an extravagant manner.

spoil
(spoyl)
VERB: To taint or ruin something; the adjective form "spoiled" means to no longer be edible because of decay.

spree
(spree)
NOUN: A period marked by some sort of self-indulgent behavior, from shopping to drinking.

squander
(SKWON-der)
VERB: To spend or diminish something in a wasteful manner.

starving
(STAR-ving)
ADJECTIVE: Extremely hungry; ravenous.

stocky
(STOK-ee)
ADJECTIVE: Being broad and somewhat overweight.

stomach
(STUHM-ick)
VERB: To tolerate something.

stout
(stowt)
ADJECTIVE: Refers to a somewhat heavy person. As a noun, it describes a very strong and dark type of beer.

stuffed
(stuhft)
ADJECTIVE: Filled with something, or the feeling of being completely full.

A collective sigh came from the table as they all sat there STUFFED from the holiday feast.

suds
(suhdz)
NOUN: Slang word for beer.

sumptuous
(SUMP-choo-us)
ADJECTIVE: Luxurious or lavish.

superfluous
(soo-PER-floo-uss)
ADJECTIVE: In excess of what is needed; unnecessary.

surfeit
(SUR-fit)
NOUN: So much of something as to make one bored or sick; as a verb, *surfeit* means to overindulge or give somebody an excessive amount of something.

sweet tooth
(SWEET tooth)
NOUN: A fondness for candy or other sweets.

swig

(swig)

NOUN: A large swallow of a beverage, particularly alcohol. As a verb, it means to swallow a beverage down quickly.

> *Drunk and merry, the old man haphazardly wandered down the sidewalk, SWIGGING from a bottle and singing to anyone he bumped into.*

swinish

(SWYN-ish)

ADJECTIVE: Suggestive of swine; hoggish.

sybarite

(SIB-uh-rahyt)

NOUN: One who devotes his or her life to the pursuit of pleasure; sensualist.

The chief beginning of evil is

goodness in excess.

—MENANDER

T

Take heed of a gluttonous

curiosity to feed on many

things, lest the greediness of

the appetite of thy memory

spoil the digestion thereof.

—Thomas Fuller

take a drop
(teyk a drop)
VERB: To drink alcohol; quaff.

thirst
(thurst)
NOUN: A dry mouth or throat that leads to the desire for a drink; any insistent desire.

Even though the couple simply lied in the sun all day, exerting no energy, they came back to the house with an insatiable THIRST.

titanic
(tie-TAN-ic)
ADJECTIVE: Having extraordinary strength, size, or power; colossal.

toss back
(toss bak)
VERB: To drink or guzzle a beverage, particularly an alcoholic one.

treat
(treet)

NOUN: An object or service—such as food or a massage—that is given as a reward, particularly when it's a surprise.

When you put no limit on your indulgences, there really is no such thing as a TREAT.

trencherman
(TREN-chur-man)

NOUN: A person with a big appetite; a big eater.

tubby
(TUB-ee)

ADJECTIVE: Chubby or overweight.

U

In general, mankind,

since the improvement of

cookery, eats twice as much

as nature requires.

—Benjamin Franklin

uncalled-for

(uhn-KAWLD-for)

ADJECTIVE: Not called for; unwarranted or unnecessary.

uncontrollable

(un-kon-TROHL-uh-buhl)

ADJECTIVE: Not able to be controlled or repressed; out of control.

> *Michael realized his need to drink had become UNCONTROLLABLE when every moment of every day was spent thinking about his next drink.*

undue

(un-DOO)

ADJECTIVE: Unwarranted or unjustified; uncalled-for.

unending

(un-END-ing)

ADJECTIVE: Without end; never-ending.

unflagging

(un-FLAG-ing)

ADJECTIVE: Unwavering; untiring.

uninhibited

(un-in-HIB-ih-ted)

ADJECTIVE: Without inhibitions or restraint; unrestrained.

unlimited

(un-LIM-ih-ted)

ADJECTIVE: Without limits or restrictions; infinite.

The manor's wine cellar boasted a seemingly UNLIMITED number of vintages, with bottles lining the walls as far as the eye could see.

unnecessary

(un-NESS-uh-sayr-ee)

ADJECTIVE: Describes something that is not necessary or needed.

unrelenting

(un-ree-LENT-ing)

ADJECTIVE: Describes something that does not give up or weaken; insistent.

unreserved

(un-ree-ZIRVD)

ADJECTIVE: Without restrictions or reservations; frank.

unrestrained

(un-ree-STREYND)

ADJECTIVE: Without restraints or controls;
uninhibited.

unrestricted

(un-ree-STRIK-ted)

ADJECTIVE: Without restrictions or hindrances;
unhampered.

unsatisfied

(un-SAT-iss-fiyd)

ADJECTIVE: Not satisfied or pleased; discontented.

unwarranted

(un-WOR-uhn-ted)

ADJECTIVE: Not warranted or justified; undeserved.

urge

(erj)

NOUN: A strong need or inclination; as a verb, to
urge is to strongly suggest or advise someone to act
in a particular way.

> *Even when he could feel his stomach becoming full,
> there was still an URGE inside Henry to keep eating, to
> clean his plate of every last delicious morsel.*

V

Bad men live to eat and

drink, whereas good men eat

and drink in order to live.

—SOCRATES

viand

(VAHY-und)

NOUN: A piece of food or the pieces of food that make up a meal; a delicious dish.

volition

(vo-LISH-un)

NOUN: A conscious choice; the act of expressing one's free will.

voluminous

(vuh-LOO-mih-nuss)

ADJECTIVE: Having great volume or capacity; large.

voluptuary

(vuh-LUP-shoo-er-ee)

NOUN: One who devotes his or her life to luxury and sensual pleasures.

A definite VOLUPTUARY, Gretta made certain that any of the food she was served sated all of her senses.

voracious

(vor-AY-shuss)

ADJECTIVE: Extremely hungry or enthusiastic—
about eating or some other activity; insatiable.

*A true gourmand may be able to satisfy his hunger,
but he always remains VORACIOUS, looking for that
next great meal.*

voracity

(vor-ASS-ih-tee)

NOUN: Gluttony or greed.

W

want

(want)

VERB: To have a desire or need for something.

watering hole

(WOT-er-ing HOHL)

NOUN: A bar or other location where people gather to drink and be social.

> *Dennis stumbled out from his favorite WATERING HOLE full of piss and vinegar—and close to a dozen pints—he was ready to take on the world.*

wastrel

(WAY-strel)

NOUN: An insulting word for a wasteful person; spendthrift.

weakness

(WEEK-nes)

NOUN: Lacking in strength or power; *weakness* can be used in reference to a person or thing that one cannot resist.

The glutton castaway, the drunkard in the desert, the lecher in prison, they are the happy ones. To hunger, thirst, lust, every day afresh and every day in vain, after the old prog, the old booze, the old whores, that's the nearest we'll ever get to felicity, the new porch and the very latest garden.

—SAMUEL BECKETT

wolf

(woolf)

VERB: To eat something very quickly and in a greedy manner.

Watching the soldiers in the mess hall eat was almost like viewing feeding time at the zoo; they hardly came up for air as they WOLFED down meat and vegetables and pasta and anything else that crossed their plates' paths.

Y and Z

yearning
(YURN-ing)

NOUN: A very strong want or desire for something, particularly something that is likely out of one's reach.

> *Beyond any thirst or hunger he ever felt before, Victor had an intense YEARNING to indulge in his favorite meal right before he was put to death.*

yen
(yehn)

NOUN: A strong urge or longing for something.

zealot
(ZEL-ut)

NOUN: One who has an excessive passion for something; fanatic.

zealous
(ZEL-us)

ADJECTIVE: Extremely enthusiastic and full of zeal.

zest
(zest)

NOUN: Enjoyment or enthusiasm; gusto.

zymurgy
(ZIE-mur-jee)
NOUN: The scientific study of fermentation in brewing processes.

DAILY BENDER

Want Some More?

Hit up our humor blog, The Daily Bender, to get your fill of all things funny—be it subversive, odd, offbeat, or just plain mean. The Bender editors are there to get you through the day and on your way to happy hour. Whether we're linking to the latest video that made us laugh or calling out (or bullshit on) whatever's happening, we've got what you need for a good laugh.

If you like our book, you'll love our blog. (And if you hated it, "man up" and tell us why.) Visit The Daily Bender for a shot of humor that'll serve you until the bartender can.